A Shame To Miss

2

Poetry collections by Anne Fine published by Corgi Books:
A SHAME TO MISS . . . 1
A SHAME TO MISS . . . 2
A SHAME TO MISS . . . 3

Published by Doubleday for older readers:

UP ON CLOUD NINE
'A real treat for the many fans of the Children's Laureate; a highly enjoyable novel
that is characteristically funny, clever and moving'
Financial Times

Other books by Anne Fine for older readers:
THE SUMMER-HOUSE LOON
THE OTHER DARKER NED
THE STONE MENAGERIE
ROUND BEHIND THE ICEHOUSE
THE GRANNY PROJECT
MADAME DOUBTFIRE
GOGGLE-EYES
THE BOOK OF THE BANSHEE
FLOUR BABIES
STEP BY WICKED STEP
THE TULIP TOUCH

Published by Doubleday / Yearling for junior readers:

CHARM SCHOOL
'A funny read which pre-teens should latch on to' *Children's Bookseller*

BAD DREAMS
'A beautifully plotted, well-told mix of fantasy thriller and closely observed
school drama' *Daily Telegraph*

www.annefine.co.uk

A Shame To Miss 2

SELECTED BY

ANNE FINE

Corgi Books

A SHAME TO MISS . . . 2
A CORGI BOOK 0552 548685

Published in Great Britain by Corgi Books,
an imprint of Random House Children's Books

This edition published 2002

1 3 5 7 9 10 8 6 4 2

Set in Palatino

Corgi Books are published by Random House Children's Books,
61–63 Uxbridge Road, London 5SA,
a division of The Random House Group Ltd,
in Australia by Random House Australia (Pty) Ltd,
20 Alfred Street, Milsons Point, Sydney, NSW 2061, Australia,
in New Zealand by Random House New Zealand Ltd,
18 Poland Road, Glenfield, Auckland 10, New Zealand,
and in South Africa by Random House (Pty) Ltd,
Endulini, 5A Jubilee Road, Parktown 2193, South Africa

THE RANDOM HOUSE GROUP Limited Reg. No. 954009
www.kidsatrandomhouse.co.uk

A CIP catalogue record for this book is available from the British Library.

Typeset by SX Composing DTP, Rayleigh, Essex
Printed and bound in Great Britain by
Bookmarque Ltd, Croydon, Surrey

Contents

For Richard

Introduction

It was a whole lot easier for people my age to come to know, and even enjoy, whole reams of poetry. For one thing, our grandparents were forever spouting great chunks of their own favourites as we sat on their knees. (I'm not kidding). They'd been forced to learn them at school or in Sunday school, either as homework or as punishments. And they were often still word perfect half a century later. One of my grandmother's party tricks was to make my poor mother weep buckets – even at forty years old – by reeling off some dismal Victorian tear-jerker about a family so poor that they had to give away one of their children, and were trying to decide which one to choose. (I've spared you that one.)

I've chosen poems people your age find easy to like. The more you say a poem aloud, the easier it is to 'unpick it' to see what it means, especially if you pay attention to the punctuation. And sometimes I've put something by the poem, so you'll understand what it's about a little more quickly.

Go on. You might enjoy them. Millions do. They can't *all* be pretending.

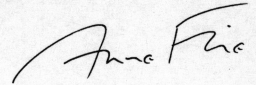

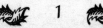

Poem: A Reminder

Capital letters prompting every line,
Lines printed down the centre of each page,
Clear spaces between groups of these, combine
In a convention of respectable age
To mean: 'Read carefully. Each word we chose
Has rhythm and sound and sense. This is
    not prose.'

Robert Graves

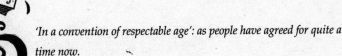

*'In a convention of respectable age': as people have agreed for quite a
time now.*

The Forbidden Play

I'll tell you the truth, Father, though your heart bleed:
    To the Play I went,
With sixpence for a near seat, money's worth indeed,
    The best ever spent.

You forbade me, you threatened me, but here's the story
    Of my splendid night:
It was colour, drums, music, a tragic glory,
    Fear with delight.

Hamlet, Prince of Denmark, title of the tale:
    He of that name,
A tall, glum fellow, velvet cloaked, with a shirt of mail,
    Two eyes like flame.

All the furies of Hell circled round that man,
    Maddening his heart,
There was old murder done before play began,
    Aye, the ghost took part.

There were grave-diggers delving, they brought up
      bones,
    And with rage and grief
All the players shouted in full, kingly tones,
    Grand, passing belief.

Ah, there were ladies there radiant as day,
    And changing scenes:
Fabulous words were tossed about like hay
    By kings and queens.

I puzzled on the sense of it in vain,
    Yet for pain I cried,
As one and all they faded, poisoned or slain,
    In great agony died.

Drive me out, Father, never to return,
    Though I am your son,
And penniless! But that glory for which I burn
    Shall be soon begun:

I shall wear great boots, shall strut and shout,
    Keep my locks curled;
The fame of my name shall go ringing about
    Over half the world.

Robert Graves

As you'll see from this, Shakespeare isn't reckoned our greatest playwright for nothing.

Earl Cassilis's Lady

Meeting her on the heath at the day's end,
After the one look and the one sigh, he said,
Did a spine prick you from the goosefeather bed?
Were the rings too heavy on your hand?
Were you unhappy, that you had to go?
No.

Was it the music called you down the stair,
Or the hot ginger that they gave you then?
Was it for pleasure that you followed them
Putting off your slippers at the door
To dance barefoot and blood-foot in the snow?
No.

What then? What glamoured you? No glamour at all;
Only that I remembered I was young
And had to put myself into a song.
How could time bear witness that I was tall,
Silken, and made for love, if I did not so?
I do not know.

Sylvia Townsend Warner

Mother to Son

Well, son, I'll tell you:
Life for me ain't been no crystal stair.
It's had tacks in it,
And splinters,
And boards torn up,
And places with no carpet on the floor –
Bare.
But all the time
I's been a-climbin' on,
And reachin' landins,
And turnin' corners,
And sometimes goin' in the dark
Where there ain't been no light.
So boy, don't you turn back.
Don't you set down on the steps
'Cause you finds it's kinder hard.
Don't you fall now –
For I's still goin', honey,
I's still climbin',
And life for me ain't been no crystal stair.

Langston Hughes

Okay, Brown Girl, Okay

For Josie, 9 years old, who wrote to me saying ' . . . boys called me names because of my colour. I felt very upset . . . How do you like being brown?'

Josie, Josie, I am okay
being brown. I remember,
every day dusk and dawn get born
from the loving of night and light
who work together, like married.
    And they would like to say to you:
    Be at school on and on, brown Josie
    like thousands and thousands and thousands
    of children, who are brown and white
    and black and pale-lemon colour.
    All the time, brown girl Josie is okay.

Josie, Josie, I am okay
being brown. I remember,
every minute sun in the sky
and ground of the earth work together
like married.
    And they would like to say to you:
    Ride on up a going escalator
    like thousands and thousands and thousands
    of people, who are brown and white
    and black and pale-lemon colour.
    All the time, brown girl Josie is okay.

Josie, Josie, I am okay
being brown. I remember,
all the time bright-sky and brown-earth
work together, like married
making forests and food and flowers and rain.
    And they would like to say to you:
    Grow and grow and brightly, brown girl.
    Write and read and play and work.
    Ride bus or train or boat or aeroplane
    like thousands and thousands and thousands
    of people, who are brown and white
    and black and pale-lemon colour.
    All the time, brown girl Josie is okay.

James Berry

Laura Round and Round

When Laura turns five cartwheels, long legs flashing,
firm hands walking green grass round her head,
bare feet singing blue sky as they tread
heavens below her, earth above her going,
all its daisies downward on her growing,
all its summer whirling with her smile –
Laura, upside-down, turns for a little while
whole worlds right side up.

Russell Hoban

You Many Big Ships with Your Billowing Sails

You many big ships with your billowing sails
   gliding out on the seas of the morning
with bright flags flying and the sailors crying
and the wild winds blowing and the wild seas flowing
   and above you the Bird of Dawning:

To France and Spain and the Spanish Main
   and the Isles of Australia turning
your golden bows as the gale allows
when the green wave slides along your sides
   and you lean as though you were yearning

For some far shore where there's no more
   cloud or sorrow or weeping:
you flaunt your great sails through the storms
   and the gales
and in the calm night ride on the bright stars as
   though you were sleeping:

Ships proud and splendid, it is never ended
   your voyage into the morning.
Though in storms and rains and wild hurricanes
you welter and wallow, you will still follow
   the beautiful Bird of Dawning.

George Barker

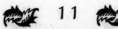

Acquainted with the Night

I have been one acquainted with the night.
I have walked out in rain – and back in rain.
I have outwalked the furthest city light.

I have looked down the saddest city lane.
I have passed by the watchman on his beat
And dropped my eyes, unwilling to explain.

I have stood still and stopped the sound of feet
When far away an interrupted cry
Came over houses from another street,

But not to call me back or say good-bye;
And further still at an unearthly height,
One luminary clock against the sky

Proclaimed the time was neither wrong nor right.
I have been one acquainted with the night.

Robert Frost

*It was my job to walk the dog, and although I never actually wanted to get
going, as soon as I was out I was perfectly happy, especially on winter nights.
For some years, this was my favourite poem.*

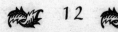

Teddy

Of course I had a Teddy; most kids did.
But most kids didn't share that stupid name:
I knew I'd been baptized after my dad
And his. Eight English kings were called the same,

Something to live up to. Oh, but *Teddy*:
I did so loathe those soppy syllables!
All my life I'd be a cuddly kiddy,
One of this hard world's inconsolables.

I murdered Teddy, pulled out both his eyes,
Pulled off a leg, an arm, ripped out some fur.
Stout *Edward* I remained, all my schooldays;
Then, grown-up, it was *Ted* that I'd prefer.

I'm ageing now. I guess he's still up there,
In mother's loft, my doleful Teddy-Bear.

Ted Walker

Keep the teddy-bears of the world safe – don't tease your local Edward!

 13

Scots Wha Hae

Scots, wha hae wi' Wallace bled,
Scots, wham Bruce has aften led,
Welcome to your gory bed,
Or to victorie.

Now's the day, and now's the hour,
See the front o' battle lour!
See approach proud Edward's power –
Chains and slaverie!

Wha will be a traitor knave?
Wha can fill a coward's grave?
Wha sae base as be a slave?
Let him turn and flee!

Wha for Scotland's King and law
Freedom's sword will strongly draw,
Freeman stand, or freeman fa'?
Let him follow me!

By oppression's woes and pains!
By your sons in servile chains!
We will drain our dearest veins,
But they shall be free!

Lay the proud usurpers low!
Tyrants fall in every foe!
Liberty's in every blow!
Let us do or die!

Robert Burns

The speech Robert Bruce might have given to his army before the Battle of Bannockburn in 1314. (The Scots, though outnumbered, roundly beat the English under Edward II.)

Scots wha hae: Scots who have
Wallace: a warrior patriot
lour: loom
fa': fall

With a Scots accent, of course, the last word of the poem rhymes with the other last lines.

from The Lady of Shalott

Everyone knows bits of this. I only have room to pick out the most famous verses, and keep you up with what little plot there is.

On either side the river lie
Long fields of barley and of rye,
That clothe the wold and meet the sky;
And thro' the field the road runs by
     To many-tower'd Camelot;
And up and down the people go,
Gazing where the lilies blow
Round an island there below,
     The island of Shalott.

The Lady of Shalott lives alone in a tower on this river island.

There she weaves by night and day
A magic web with colours gay.
She has heard a whisper say,
A curse is on her if she stay
     To look down to Camelot.
She knows not what the curse may be,
And so she weaveth steadily,
And little other care hath she,
     The Lady of Shalott.

And moving thro' a mirror clear
That hangs before her all the year,
Shadows of the world appear.
There she sees the highway near
       Winding down to Camelot . . .

* * *

. . . And sometimes thro' the mirror blue
The knights come riding two and two:
She hath no loyal knight and true,
       The Lady of Shalott.

But in her web she still delights
To weave the mirror's magic sights,
For often thro' the silent nights
A funeral, with plumes and lights
       And music, went to Camelot:
Or when the moon was overhead,
Came two young lovers lately wed;
'I am half sick of shadows,' said
       The Lady of Shalott.

* * *

And then, one day, she sees Sir Lancelot riding by...

His broad clear brow in sunlight glow'd;
On burnish'd hooves his war-horse trode;
From underneath his helmet flow'd
His coal-black curls as on he rode,
     As he rode down to Camelot.

From the bank and from the river
He flash'd into the crystal mirror,
'Tirra lirra,' by the river
     Sang Sir Lancelot.

She left the web, she left the loom,
She made three paces thro' the room,
She saw the water-lily bloom,
She saw the helmet and the plume,
     She look'd down to Camelot.
Out flew the web and floated wide;
The mirror crack'd from side to side;
'The curse is come upon me,' cried
     The Lady of Shalott.

I won't spoil the ending. (It isn't much of one, anyway.)

Alfred, Lord Tennyson

(with apologies)

The Frog and the Golden Ball

She let her golden ball fall down the well
    And begged a cold frog to retrieve it;
For which she kissed his ugly, gaping mouth –
    Indeed, he could scarce believe it.

And seeing him transformed to his princely shape,
    Who had been by hags enchanted,
She knew she could never love another man
    Nor by any fate be daunted.

But what would her royal father and mother say?
    They had promised her in marriage
To a cousin whose wide kingdom marched with theirs,
    Who rode in a jewelled carriage.

'Our plight, dear heart, would appear past human hope
    To all but you and me: in fact to all
Who have never swum as a frog in a dark well
    Or have lost a golden ball.'

'What then shall we do now?' she asked her lover.
    He kissed her again and said:
'Is magic of love less powerful at your Court
    Than at this green well-head?'

Robert Graves

Come From That
Window Child

For Pat Rodney and her children, and the other
thousands in whom Walter Rodney* lives on.

Come from that window child
no use looking for daddy tonight
daddy not coming home tonight

Come from that window child
all you'll see is stars burning bright
you won't ever see daddy car light

Come from that window child
in your heart I know you asking why
in my heart too I wish the news was lie

Come from that window child
tonight I feel the darkness bleed
can't tell flower from seed

Come from that window child
to live for truth ain't no easy fight
when some believe power is their right

Come from that window child
a bomb blow up daddy car tonight
but daddy words still burning bright

Come from that window child
tonight you turn a man before your time
tonight you turn a man before your time

John Agard

Walter Rodney, a Guyanese historian and revolutionary and author of How
Europe Underdeveloped Africa, *was killed on 13 October 1980 in Guyana.*

The Highwayman

The wind was a torrent of darkness among the gusty
     trees,
The moon was a ghostly galleon tossed upon cloudy
     seas,
The road was a ribbon of moonlight over the purple
     moor,
And the highwayman came riding –
    Riding – riding –
The highwayman came riding, up to the old inn-door.

He'd a French cocked-hat on his forehead, a bunch of
     lace at his chin,
A coat of claret velvet, and breeches of brown doe-skin;
They fitted with never a wrinkle: his boots were up to
     the thigh!
And he rode with a jewelled twinkle,
    His pistol butts a-twinkle,
His rapier hilt a-twinkle, under the jewelled sky.

Over the cobbles he clattered and clashed in the dark
     inn-yard,
And he tapped with his whip on the shutters, but all
     was locked and barred;
He whistled a tune to the window, and who should be
     waiting there
But the landlord's black-eyed daughter,
    Bess, the landlord's daughter,
Plaiting a dark red love-knot into her long black hair.

And dark in the old inn-yard a stable-wicket creaked
Where Tim the ostler listened; his face was white and
     peaked;
His eyes were hollows of madness, his hair like
     mouldy hay,
But he loved the landlord's daughter,
    The landlord's red-lipped daughter;
Dumb as a dog he listened, and he heard the robber say –

'One kiss, my bonny sweetheart, I'm after a prize
     to-night,
But I shall be back with the yellow gold before the
     morning light;
Yet, if they press me sharply, and harry me through
     the day,
Then look for me by moonlight,
    Watch for me by moonlight,
I'll come to thee by moonlight, though hell should bar
     the way.'

He rose upright in the stirrups; he scarce could reach
     her hand,
But she loosened her hair i' the casement! His face
     burnt like a brand
As the black cascade of perfume came tumbling over
     his breast;
And he kissed its waves in the moonlight,
    (Oh, sweet black waves in the moonlight!)
Then he tugged at his rein in the moonlight, and
     galloped away to the west.

II

He did not come in the dawning; he did not come at noon;
And out o' the tawny sunset, before the rise o' the moon,
When the road was a gipsy's ribbon, looping the
      purple moor,
A red-coat troop came marching –
      Marching – marching –
King George's men came marching, up to the old inn-
      door.

They said no word to the landlord, they drank his ale
      instead,
But they gagged his daughter and bound her to the
      foot of her narrow bed;
Two of them knelt at her casement, with muskets at
      their side!
There was death at every window;
      And hell at one dark window;
For Bess could see, through her casement, the road
      that *he* would ride.

They had tied her up to attention, with many a
      sniggering jest;
They had bound a musket beside her, with the barrel
      beneath her breast!
'Now keep good watch!' and they kissed her.
      She heard the dead man say –
Look for me by moonlight;
      Watch for me by moonlight;

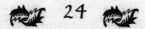

I'll come to thee by moonlight, though hell should bar the way!

She twisted her hands behind her; but all the knots
    held good!
She writhed her hands till her fingers were wet with
    sweat or blood!
They stretched and strained in the darkness, and the
    hours crawled by like years,
Till, now, on the stroke of midnight,
    Cold, on the stroke of midnight,
The tip of one finger touched it! The trigger at least
    was hers!

The tip of one finger touched it; she strove no more for
    the rest!
Up, she stood to attention, with the barrel beneath her
    breast,
She would not risk their hearing; she would not strive
    again;
For the road lay bare in the moonlight;
    Blank and bare in the moonlight;
And the blood of her veins in the moonlight throbbed
    to her love's refrain.

Tlot-tlot; tlot-tlot! Had they heard it? The horse-hoofs
    ringing clear;
Tlot-tlot, tlot-tlot, in the distance? Were they deaf that
    they did not hear?
Down the ribbon of moonlight, over the brow of the hill,
The highwayman came riding,

 25

Riding, riding!
The red-coats looked to their priming! She stood up,
    straight and still!

Tlot-tlot, in the frosty silence! *tlot-tlot*, in the echoing
    night!
Nearer he came and nearer! Her face was like a light!
Her eyes grew wide for a moment; she drew one last
    deep breath,
Then her finger moved in the moonlight,
    Her musket shattered the moonlight,
Shattered her breast in the moonlight and warned him
    – with her death.

He turned; he spurred to the westward; he did not
    know who stood
Bowed, with her head o'er the musket, drenched with
    her own red blood!
Not till the dawn he heard it, and slowly blanched to hear
How Bess, the landlord's daughter,
    The landlord's black-eyed daughter,
Had watched for her love in the moonlight, and died
    in the darkness there.

Back, he spurred like a madman, shrieking a curse to
    the sky,
With the white road smoking behind him and his
    rapier brandished high!
Blood-red were his spurs i' the golden noon; wine-red
    was his velvet coat;

When they shot him down on the highway,
    Down like a dog on the highway,
And he lay in his blood on the highway, with the
      bunch of lace at his throat.

And still of a winter's night, they say, when the wind is in
    the trees,
When the moon is a ghostly galleon tossed upon cloudy seas,
When the road is a ribbon of moonlight over the purple moor,
A highwayman comes riding –
    Riding – riding –
A highwayman comes riding, up to the old inn-door.

Over the cobbles he clatters and clangs in the dark inn-yard
And he taps with his whip on the shutters, but all is locked
    and barred;
He whistles a tune to the window, and who should be
    waiting there
But the landlord's black-eyed daughter,
    Bess, the landlord's daughter,
Plaiting a dark red love-knot into her long black hair.

Alfred Noyes

ostler: stableman
casement: window
priming gunpowder: getting ready to fire
blanched: went pale

Take One Home for the Kiddies

On shallow straw, in shadeless glass,
Huddled by empty bowls, they sleep:
No dark, no dam, no earth, no grass –
Mam, get us one of them to keep.

Living toys are something novel,
But it soon wears off somehow.
Fetch the shoebox, fetch the shovel –
Mam, we're playing funerals now.

Philip Larkin

dam: mother

novel: new

This has to be the toughest 'a pet is not just for Christmas' poem ever.

The Twelve Dancing Princesses

In later life, none could recapture
  that long season of dancing nights –
    the enchanted risk of them:
      at twelve, the flight down steps;
        silk dresses rustling through groves
          of gold, diamond, and silver
            to the boat trip on moon-filmed water,
          the lake sighing and whispering its secrets
        as their perfect princes rowed them
      towards the underground castle
then danced the soles out of their shoes
    and plied them with wine
      and were impeccable
        as they rowed them home
          silent with ecstasy
            over the pear-shaped lake –
          princesses with dancing eyes
        returning to their locked room.
      Only the soldier who'd shadowed them,
    who'd stepped on the hem of the youngest
(her half-lit face half-turned)
    brought back mementos –
      three precious twigs and
        one of the goblets he'd emptied
          while partnering each princess
            invisibly, in his magic cloak.
            Then the exposé, the opulent evidence . . .
      The eldest was forced to marry him,

 29

the others became royal wives
in far kingdoms where they had
balls and ballgowns to order.
They glittered with riches
and smiled convincingly
but never again would they
dance their slippers through.
Strange jewellery they had made –
gold leaves veined with diamonds
and tiny silver twigs that they wore
like open secrets. Often, too,
they remembered the lantern
that sung across the lake
as if a star were caged in it.
In the cellar of the first castle
were heaped all the dancing shoes
full of centipedes and mice
and ropes of dust and mouldering
wine from a leaky cask
and old newspapers, sere
as parchment, and a book
with a rusty lock, containing
stories that sometimes ended,
'and the mouth of the last person
who told this story is still warm'.

Diane Fahey

impeccable: *perfectly well-mannered*
exposé: *the secret coming out*
opulent: *rich*

Because I have four sisters, everyone was always saying, 'Five girls! Fancy!' So
The Twelve Dancing Princesses was my favourite fairytale. It made me feel
more normal. And I often wondered how things must have worked out
afterwards . . .

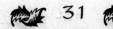

Hunter Trials

It's awf'lly bad luck on Diana,
    Her ponies have swallowed their bits;
She fished down their throats with a spanner
    And frightened them all into fits.

So now she's attempting to borrow.
    Do lend her some bits, Mummy, *do*;
I'll lend her my own for to-morrow,
    But to-day, *I*'ll be wanting them too.

Just look at Prunella on Guzzle,
    The wizardest pony on earth;
Why doesn't she slacken his muzzle
    And tighten the breech in his girth?

I say, Mummy, there's Mrs Geyser
    And doesn't she look pretty sick?
I bet it's because Mona Lisa
    Was hit on the hock with a brick.

Miss Blewitt says Monica threw it,
    But Monica says it was Joan,
And Joan's very thick with Miss Blewitt,
    So Monica's sulking alone.

And Margaret failed in her paces,
    Her withers got tied in a noose,
So her coronets caught in the traces
    And now all her fetlocks are loose.

Oh, it's me now. I'm terribly nervous.
    I wonder if Smudges will shy.
She's practically certain to swerve as
    Her Pelham is over one eye.

* * *

Oh wasn't it naughty of Smudges?
    Oh, Mummy, I'm sick with disgust.
She threw me in front of the Judges,
    And my silly old collarbone's bust.

John Betjeman

An Inconvenience

Mama,
papa,
and us
10 kids
lived in
a single room.
Once, when I
got sick
and like to die,
I heard a cry
slice through the gloom
'Hotdog!
We gon have
mo room!'

John Raven

I certainly hope it was neither of his parents saying it!

Snail

Enjoys the damp. Remembers smell of sea.
Once moved with fish, swaying anemone,
the steady knock and whisper of the swell.
Coiled now in dead and mottled shell,
boneless and moist, peering with pimple-eyes,
creature of chilly dawn, the soft moonrise.
And with what slow and persevering toil
he plots his route along the easy soil,
sampling each tangled leaf and dewy stem,
writing in slimy signs his requiem,
until when summer's burning finger warns,
he probes the air with dry, and anxious horns
and then his final exploration past,
discards his china house and home at last.

Leonard Clark

The natural history of this is a bit suspect, but it's a lovely poem.

 35

Fragment of an English Opera

(Designed as a model for young librettists)

Dramatis personae:
Father (bass)
Mother (contralto)
Daughter (soprano)

Scene: a room. *Time*: evening

Father:	Retire, my daughter;
	Prayers have been said;
	Take your warm water
	And go to bed.
Daughter:	But I had rather
	Sit up instead.
Father:	I am your father,
	So go to bed.
Daughter:	Are you my father?
Father:	I think so, rather:
	You go to bed.

Mother:	My daughter, vanish;
	You hear me speak:
	This is not Spanish,
	Nor is it Greek.

Daughter:	Oh, what a bother!
	Would I were dead!

Mother:	I am your mother, So go to bed.
Daughter:	Are you my mother?
Mother:	You have no other: You go to bed.
Father:	Take your bed-candle And take it quick. This is the handle.
Daughter:	Is *this* the handle?

Father:	No, that's the wick.
	This is the handle,
	    At this end here.
	Take your bed-candle
	    And disappear.

Daughter:	Oh, dear, oh dear!

Father &
Mother:
	Take your warm water,
	    As we have said;
	You are our daughter,
	    So go to bed.

Daughter:	Am I your daughter?
Father & *Mother*:	If not, you oughter: You go to bed.
Daughter:	I am their daughter; If not, I oughter: Prayers have been said. This is my mother;

I have no other:
    Would I were dead!
That is my father;
He thinks so, rather:
    Oh dear, oh dear!
I take my candle;
This is the handle:
    I disappear.

Father &
Mother: The coast is clear.

A. E. Housman

This does tend to be how the words in an opera (the libretto) unravel.
So it's good that it's the music that's the important thing.

 38

In the Public Library

The infant, while his mother peers at novels,
Sings of a black sheep and its cry and fleece.
She doesn't seem to worry that he grovels
In mucky footprints and the parquet's grease.

I have to step across the raucous singer
(Anorak making him still more obese).
I could, but don't, tread on his grubby finger;
Though let him see my face – a cruel crook's.

I only hope his life will gain from books.

Roy Fuller

parquet: *wooden floor*
raucous: *noisy*
obese: *tubby*

This poem really unnerves me as this could be any child of mine. Still, at least
the last line's a comfort: their lives have very definitely gained from books.

Hey There Now!

(For Lesley)

Hey there now
my brownwater flower
    my sunchild branching
from my mountain river
    hey there now!
my young stream
      headlong
        rushing
I love to watch you
    when you're
    sleeping
      blushing

Grace Nichols

The Road Not Taken

Two roads diverged in a yellow wood,
And sorry I could not travel both
And be one traveler, long I stood
And looked down one as far as I could
To where it bent in the undergrowth;

Then took the other, as just as fair,
And having perhaps the better claim,
Because it was grassy and wanted wear;
Though as for that the passing there
Had worn them really about the same,

And both that morning equally lay
In leaves no step had trodden black.
Oh, I kept the first for another day!
Yet knowing how way leads on to way,
I doubted if I should ever come back.

I shall be telling this with a sigh
Somewhere ages and ages hence:
Two roads diverged in a wood, and I –
I took the one less traveled by,
And that has made all the difference.

Robert Frost

I met this poem the year I had to choose my exam subjects at school. It was its sheer wistfulness that appealed to me then, and it means even more now.

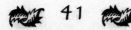

Mother, I cannot mind my wheel

Mother, I cannot mind my wheel;
　My fingers ache, my lips are dry;
Oh! if you felt the pain I feel!
　But oh, who ever felt as I?

Sappho
translated by Walter Savage Landor

mind my wheel: pay attention to my spinning

We only have scraps of Sappho's poetry, but they have been enough to inspire other poets for centuries. She lived on the Greek island of Lesbos between 630 and 612 BC. (The numbers go backwards because, in BC – Before Christ – we're counting down to AD – Anno Domini, or the Year of Our Lord.)

Song of a Chaste Wife

You knew, sir, that I had a husband,
When you sent me this pair of shining pearls.
Grateful for your skein-soft thoughts,
I wore them over my red gauze bodice.
But my home is a tall house built beside the Imperial
    grounds,
And my good man bears arms in the Palace of Radiance.
I know, sir, that your heart is pure as the sun and the
    moon.
But in serving my husband I have vowed to be with
    him in life and death;
So I now return your two shining pearls with a tear on
    each,
Regretting that we did not meet while I was still unwed.

Chang Chi

skein-soft: soft as yarn

Fatima

Class, this is Fatima
all the way from –
who can spell Bosnia for me?

I know if she could speak
English, she would tell us
what a lucky girl she feels
to be here in Bromley – THIS IS BROMLEY –
while all her friends
had to stay behind in –
who can spell Sarajevo for me?

This morning we are going to carry on
with our Nativity Play For Today.
Fatima has lovely blonde hair – HAIR –
so she is going to play the Virgin Mary;
then she won't have to say anything.
No sulking, Lisa; you can be
the landlady. She's got a nice rude speech
and a shiny handbag.

Alex is Joseph; you other boys
are soldiers. But remember
you're not to get carried away
killing the babies. This is acting.

Fatima, sit here, dear;
this is your baby – BABY.
Joseph, put your hand on her shoulder.
Now, angel chorus, let's have the first verse
of 'Hope for the world, peace evermore.'
Herod, stop fidgeting with your kalashnikov.
Fatima, why are you crying?

Carole Satyamurti

*Thousands of refugee children arrived during the Bosnian war. It's hard to bear
in mind the sights they've seen. (A Kalashnikov is a gun.)*

This poem looks impossible but it's really a good laugh. The turkey's just realized that Christmas is coming and if he's not careful, he won't see New Year. If a word defeats you, try saying it aloud. You'll soon get the knack. I've given explanations of some of the words on the following page.

Soliloquy of a Turkey

Dey's a so't o' threatenin' feelin' in de blowin' of de
    breeze,
  An' I's feelin' kin' o' squeamish in de night;
I's a walkin' 'roun' a-lookin' at de diffunt style o' trees,
  An' a-measurin' dey thickness an' dey height.
Fu' dey's somep'n mighty 'spicious in de looks de
    da'kies give,
  Ez day pass me an' my fambly in de groun',
So it 'curs to me dat lakly, ef I caihs to try an' live,
  It concehns me fu' to 'mence to look erroun'.

Dey's a cu'ious kin' o' shivah runnin' up an' down my
    back,
  An' I feel my feddahs rufflin' all de day,
An' my laigs commence to trimble evah blessid step I
    mek;
  W'en I sees a ax, I tu'ns my head away.
Folks is go'gin' me wid goodies, an' dey's treatin' me
    wid caih,
  An' I's fat in spite of all dat I kin do.
I's mistrus'ful of de kin'ness dat's erroun' me evahwhaih,
  Fu' it's jes' too good, an' frequent, to be true.

 46

Snow's a-fallin' on de medders, all erroun' me now is
   white,
   But I's still kep' on a-roostin' on de fence;
Isham comes an' feels my breas'-bone, an' he hefted
   me las' night,
   An' he's gone erroun' a-grinnin' evah sence.
'T ain't de snow dat meks me shivah; 't ain't de col'
   dat meks me shake;
   'T ain't de wintah-time itse'f dat's 'fectin' me;
But I t'ink de time is comin', an' I'd bettah mek a break,
   Fu' to set wid Mistah Possum in his tree.

W'en you hyeah de da'kies singin', an' de quahtahs
   all is gay,
   'T ain't de time fu' birds lak me to be 'erroun';
W'en de hick'ry chips is flyin', an' de log's been ca'ied
   erway,
   Den hit's dang'ous to be roostin' nigh de groun'.

Grin on, Isham! Sing on, da'kies! But I flop my wings
   an' go
   Fu' de sheltah of de ve'y highest tree,
Fu' dey's too much close ertention – an' dey's too
   much fallin' snow –
   An' it's too nigh Chris'mus mo'nin' now fu' me.

Paul Laurence Dunbar

a soliloquy: talking to yourself out loud

da'kies: historical slang referring to plantation workers

heft: lift to weigh

quahtahs: sleeping quarters

hickory chips: the perfect wood for roasting birds

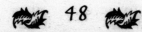

Uniform

'You'll grow,' she said and that was that. No use
To argue and to sulk invited slaps.
The empty shoulders drooped, the sleeves hung loose –
No use – she nods and the assistant wraps.

New blazer, new school socks and all between
Designed for pea pod anonymity.
All underwear the regulation green;
Alike there's none to envy, none to pity.

At home she feasts on pins. She tacks and tucks
Takes in the generous seams and smiles at thrift.
I fidget as she fits. She tuts and clucks.
With each neat stitch she digs a deeper rift.

They'll mock me with her turnings and her hem
And laugh and know that I'm not one of them.

Jan Dean

How to Grow Up

Hold on to everything horrible.
Jettison everything nice.
When you are shown something beautiful
Look at the price.

Eat something boring for breakfast.
Watch television all night.
Stop being scared of the darkness.
Start being scared of the light.

Start liking money for money's sake,
Not for what money can do.
Never look out of an aeroplane.
Always complain to the crew.

Make yourself glummer and glummer.
Spend your time scowling and be,
Smack in the middle of summer,
A grumpy old bastard like me.

Kevin McGee

from A Shropshire Lad

XVIII

Oh, when I was in love with you,
Then I was clean and brave,
And miles around the wonder grew
How well I did behave.

And now the fancy passes by
And nothing will remain,
And miles around they'll say that I
Am quite myself again.

A. E. Housman

O What Is That Sound?

O what is that sound which so thrills the ear
   Down in the valley, drumming, drumming?
Only the scarlet soldiers, dear,
   The soldiers coming.

O what is that light I see flashing so clear
   Over the distance brightly, brightly?
Only the sun on their weapons, dear,
   As they step lightly.

O what are they doing with all that gear,
   What are they doing this morning, this morning?
Only their usual manoeuvres, dear,
   Or perhaps a warning.

O why have they left the road down there,
   Why are they suddenly wheeling, wheeling?
Perhaps a change in their orders, dear.
   Why are you kneeling?

O haven't they stopped for the doctor's care,
   Haven't they reined their horses, their horses?
Why, they are none of them wounded, dear,
   None of these forces.

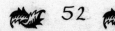

O is it the parson they want, with white hair,
    Is it the parson, is it, is it?
No, they are passing his gateway, dear,
    Without a visit.

O it must be the farmer who lives so near.
    It must be the farmer so cunning, so cunning?
They have passed the farmyard already, dear,
    And now they are running.

O where are you going? Stay with me here!
    Were the vows you swore deceiving, deceiving?
No, I promised to love you, dear,
    But I must be leaving.

O it's broken the lock and splintered the door,
    O it's the gate where they're turning, turning;
Their boots are heavy on the floor
    And their eyes are burning.

W. H. Auden

manoeuvres: army exercises

The General

'Good morning; good morning!' the General said
When we met him last week on our way to the line.
Now the soldiers he smiled at are most of 'em dead,
And we're cursing his staff for incompetent swine.
'He's a cheery old card,' grunted Harry to Jack
As they slogged up to Arras with rifle and pack.

But he did for them both by his plan of attack.

Siegfried Sassoon

In all, the Great War of 1914–18 cost 10 million lives. In my encyclopaedia
when I was a child, I had two photographs of Arras Town Hall: the first as one of
the most beautiful buildings in France, the other as a heap of rubble.

Easter Monday
(*In Memoriam E.T.*)

In the last letter that I had from France
You thanked me for the silver Easter egg
Which I had hidden in the box of apples
You liked to munch beyond all other fruit.
You found the egg the Monday before Easter,
And said, 'I will praise Easter Monday now –
It was such a lovely morning.' Then you spoke
Of the coming battle and said, 'This is the eve.
Good-bye. And may I have a letter soon.'

That Easter Monday was a day for praise,
It was such a lovely morning. In our garden
We sowed our earliest seeds, and in the orchard
The apple-bud was ripe. It was the eve.
There are three letters that you will not get.

Eleanor Farjeon

In Memoriam *means written for someone who has died. My great-grandmother
lost three sons in this war. She said the black-edged telegrams bringing the bad
news were at least half-expected. But the later return of letters that hadn't been
delivered in time was, on each occasion, the most awful shock.*

In Flanders Fields

In Flanders fields the poppies blow
Between the crosses, row on row,
   That mark our place; and in the sky
   The larks, still bravely singing, fly
Scarce heard amid the guns below.

We are the Dead. Short days ago
We lived, felt dawn, saw sunset glow,
   Loved and were loved, and now we lie
   In Flanders fields.

Take up our quarrel with the foe:
To you from failing hands we throw
   The torch; be yours to hold it high.
   If ye break faith with us who die
We shall not sleep, though poppies grow
   In Flanders fields.

John McCrae

Everyone Sang

Everyone suddenly burst out singing;
And I was filled with such delight
As prisoned birds must find in freedom
Winging wildly across the white
Orchards and dark-green fields; on – on –
   and out of sight,

Everyone's voice was suddenly lifted,
And beauty came like the setting sun.
My heart was shaken with tears; and horror
Drifted away . . . O but Everyone
Was a bird; and the song was wordless;
   the singing will never be done.

Siegfried Sassoon
April 1919

And finally, by agreement on the eleventh hour of the eleventh day of the
eleventh month (11 November 1918), everyone fighting the First World War
laid down their arms (the Armistice). The anniversary of this date now falls on
the nearest Sunday – Remembrance Sunday.

The Boyhood of Dracula

So we let him join us
In the game of Hide and Seek
Because Joanna said we ought,
She being the biggest of us all
And bossy with it.
And him standing there
All hunched and trembling
In the thin snow by the stable door
Watching us like some poor lost soul
With those great eyes he had.
Well, you'd be a thing of stone
To take no pity on the boy.
You never saw a soul
So pale and woebegone;
His pinched nose raw with cold
And naught to keep the bitter wind
The right side of his bones
But that old bit of musty cloak
He always seems to wear.

Poor little mite
You'd think, to watch,
He'd never played the game before.

Maureen Cantelow,
The parson's youngest girl
From Norton Campion way,
She found him straight away
Hardly bothering to hide at all
Among the meal sacks
In the lower barn.

Poor girl,
She must have cut herself
In there somehow
For as I spied them
Running hand in hand below
She sowed fresh seeds of crimson blood
Across ridged and bitter snow.

Gareth Owen

What Are Heavy?

What are heavy? Sea-sand and sorrow;
What are brief? Today and tomorrow;
What are frail? Spring blossoms and youth;
What are deep? The ocean and truth.

Christina Rossetti

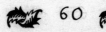

from A Shropshire Lad

XIII

When I was one-and-twenty
I heard a wise man say,
'Give crowns and pounds and guineas
But not your heart away;
Give pearls away and rubies
But keep your fancy free.'
But I was one-and-twenty,
No use to talk to me.

When I was one-and-twenty
I heard him say again,
'The heart out of the bosom
Was never given in vain;
'Tis paid with sighs a plenty
And sold for endless rue.'
And I am two-and-twenty,
And oh, 'tis true, 'tis true.

A. E. Housman

rue: regret, sorrow

Every Day in Every Way

*(Dr Coué: Every day in every way I grow
better and better)*

When I got up this morning
I thought the whole thing through:
Thought, Who's the hero, the man of the day?
Christopher, it's you.

With my left arm I raised my right arm
High above my head:
Said, Christopher, you're the greatest.
Then I went back to bed.

I wrapped my arms around me,
No use counting sheep.
I counted legions of myself
Walking on the deep.

The sun blazed on the miracle,
The blue ocean smiled:
We like the way you operate,
Frankly, we like your style.

Dreamed I was in a meadow,
Angels singing hymns,
Fighting the nymphs and shepherds
Off my holy limbs.

A girl leaned out with an apple,
Said, You can taste for free.
I never touch the stuff, dear,
I'm keeping myself for me.

Dreamed I was in heaven,
God said, Over to you,
Christopher, you're the greatest!
And Oh, it's true, it's true!

I like my face in the mirror,
I like my voice when I sing.
My girl says it's just infatuation –
I know it's the real thing.

Kit Wright

Dr Coué was one of the first 'self-help' people. He told everyone to stand in front of the mirror each morning and say this sentence.

Divorce

I did not promise
to stay with you till death us do part, or
anything like that,
so part I must, and quickly. There are things
I cannot suffer
any longer: Mother, you have never, ever, said
a kind word
or a thank you for all the tedious chores I have done;
Father, your breath
smells like a camel's and gives me the hump;
all you ever say is:
'Are you off in the cream puff, Lady Muck?'
In this day and age?
I would be better off in an orphanage.

I want a divorce.
There are parents in the world whose faces turn
up to the light
who speak in a soft murmur of rivers
and never shout.
There are parents who stroke their children's cheeks
in the dead night
and sing in the colourful voices of rainbows,
red to blue.

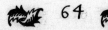

These parents are not you. I never chose you.
You are rough and wild,
I don't want to be your child. All you do is shout
and that's not right.
I will file for divorce in the morning at first light.

Jackie Kay

Love

To escape from thoughts of love,
I put on my fur-cloak,
And ran out from the lamp-lit silent house.

On a tiny footpath
The bright moon peeps:
And the withered twigs on the snow-clad earth
Across and across, everywhere scrawl 'Love'.

Ping Hsin

Today

Today I will not live up to my potential.
Today I will not relate well to my peer group.
Today I will not contribute in class.
   I will not volunteer one thing.
Today I will not strive to do better.
Today I will not achieve or adjust or grow enriched
   or get involved.
I will not put up my hand even if the teacher is
   wrong and I can prove it.

Today I might eat the eraser off my pencil.
I'll look at the clouds.
I'll be late.
I don't think I'll wash.

I need a rest.

Jean Little

from As You Like It

(*Act II, Scene vii*)

All the world's a stage,
And all the men and women merely players:
They have their exits and their entrances;
And one man in his time plays many parts,
His acts being seven ages. At first the infant,
Mewling and puking in the nurse's arms.
And then the whining schoolboy, with his satchel,
And shining morning face, creeping like snail
Unwillingly to school. And then the lover,
Sighing like furnace, with a woeful ballad
Made to his mistress' eyebrow. Then a soldier,
Full of strange oaths, and bearded like the pard,
Jealous in honour, sudden and quick in quarrel,
Seeking the bubble reputation
Even in the cannon's mouth. And then the justice,
In fair round belly with good capon lin'd,
With eyes severe, and beard of formal cut,
Full of wise saws and modern instances;
And so he plays his part. The sixth age shifts
Into the lean and slipper'd pantaloon,
With spectacles on nose and paunch on side,
His youthful hose well sav'd, a world too wide
For his shrunk shank; and his big manly voice,

Turning again toward childish treble, pipes
And whistles in his sound. Last scene of all,
That ends this strange eventful history,
Is second childishness and mere oblivion,
Sans teeth, sans eyes, sans taste, sans everything.

William Shakespeare

pard: *old word for leopard*
sans: *french for without*

*You're in Act Two. I'm moving from Act Four to Act Five. He's not very
complimentary about any of us.*

from A Shropshire Lad

VIII

'Farewell to barn and stack and tree,
    Farewell to Severn shore.
Terence, look your last at me,
    For I come home no more.

'The sun burns on the half-mown hill,
    By now the blood is dried;
And Maurice amongst the hay lies still
    And my knife is in his side.

'My mother thinks us long away;
    'Tis time the field were mown.
She had two sons at rising day,
    To-night she'll be alone.

'And here's a bloody hand to shake,
    And oh, man, here's good-bye;
We'll sweat no more on scythe and rake,
    My bloody hands and I.

'I wish you strength to bring you pride,
    And a love to keep you clean,
And I wish you luck, come Lammastide
    At racing on the green.

'Long for me the rick will wait,
    And long will wait the fold,
And long will stand the empty plate,
    And dinner will be cold.'

A. E. Housman

rick: haystack
fold: sheep pen

Tarantella

Do you remember an Inn,
Miranda?
Do you remember an Inn?
And the tedding and the spreading
Of the straw for a bedding,
And the fleas that tease in the High Pyrenees,
And the wine that tasted of the tar,
And the cheers and the jeers of the young muleteers
(Under the dark of the vine verandah)?
Do you remember an Inn,
Miranda?
Do you remember an Inn?
And the cheers and the jeers of the young muleteers
Who hadn't got a penny,
And who weren't paying any,
And the hammers at the doors and the Din?

And the Hip! Hop! Hap!
Of the clap
Of the hands to the twirl and the swirl
Of the girl gone chancing,
Glancing,
Dancing,
Backing and advancing,
Snapping of the clapper to the spin
Out and in –
And the Ting, Tong, Tang of the Guitar!

Do you remember an Inn,
Miranda?
Do you remember an Inn?
Never more,
Miranda,
Never more.
Only the high peaks hoar:
And Aragon a torrent at the door.
No sound
In the walls of the Halls where falls
The tread
Of the feet of the dead to the ground.
No sound:
Only the boom
Of the far Waterfall like Doom.

Hilaire Belloc

Have you read it? Now, if I tell you that Miranda was Captain Miranda, a fellow officer, try reading it again. This tarantella is a fast dance with castanets, the Pyrenees are mountains and Aragon is in Spain.

Lincolnshire Bomber Station

Across the road the homesick Romans made
The ground-mist thickens to a milky shroud;
Through flat, damp fields call sheep, mourning their dead
In cracked and timeless voices, unutterably sad,
Suffering for all the world, in Lincolnshire.

And I wonder how the Romans liked it here;
Flat fields, no sun, the muddy misty dawn,
And always, above all, the mad rain dripping down,
Rusting sword and helmet, wetting the feet
And soaking to the bone, down to the very heart.

Henry Treece

Personally, I like damp, grey weather. But once, during a talk at school, my elder daughter burst into tears and was, for a while, inconsolable. Like the homesick Roman soldiers in this poem, she'd spent her early childhood in a warm country, and one of the slides, showing bougainvillea blossoms tumbling over a bright sunlit wall, had triggered real grief. I felt terrible. Terrible.

A Song for England

An' a so de rain a-fall
An' a so de snow a-rain

An' a so de fog a-fall
An' a so de sun a-fail

An' a so de seasons mix
An' a so de bag-o'-tricks

But a so me understan'
De misery o' de Englishman.

Andrew Salkey

Andrew Salkey grew up in sunny Jamaica. Need I say more?

 75

The Ruined Maid

'O 'Melia, my dear, this does everything crown!
Who could have supposed I should meet you in Town?
And whence such fair garments, such prosperi-ty?' –
'O didn't you know I'd been ruined,' said she.

– 'You left us in tatters, without shoes or socks,
Tired of digging potatoes, and spudding up docks;
And now you've gay bracelets and bright feathers
    three!' –
'Yes: that's how we dress when we're ruined,' said she.

– 'At home in the barton you said "thee" and "thou",
And "thik oon", and "theäs oon", and "t'other"; but now
Your talking quite fits 'ee for high compa-ny!'
'Some polish is gained with one's ruin,' said she.

– 'Your hands were like paws then, your face blue and
    bleak
But now I'm bewitched by your delicate cheek,
And your little gloves fit as on any la-dy!' –
'We never do work when we're ruined,' said she.

– 'You used to call home-life, a hag-ridden dream,
And you'd sigh, and you'd sock; but at present you seem
To know not of megrims or melancho-ly' –
'True. One's pretty lively when ruined,' said she.

– 'I wish I had feathers, a fine sweeping gown,
And a delicate face, and could strut about Town!' –
'My dear – a raw country girl, such as you be,
Cannot quite expect that. You ain't ruined,' said she.

Thomas Hardy

I love this. It's so pert.

spudding up docks: weeding with a hoe
in the barton: on the farm
sigh and sock: pine and sigh
megrims: low moods

from The Rubáiyát of Omar Khayyám

(18–23)

I sometimes think that never blows so red
The rose as where some buried Caesar bled;
That every hyacinth the garden wears
Dropped in her lap from some once lovely head.

And this reviving herb whose tender green
Fledges the river's lip on which we lean –
Ah, lean upon it lightly! for who knows
From what once lovely lip it springs unseen!

Ah, my beloved, fill the cup that clears
Today of past regrets and future fears:
Tomorrow! Why, tomorrow I may be
Myself with yesterday's seven thousand years:

For some we loved, the loveliest and the best
That from his vintage rolling Time hath prest,
Have drunk their cup a round or two before,
And one by one crept silently to rest.

And we, that now make merry in the room
They left, and Summer dresses in new bloom,
Ourselves must we beneath the couch of earth
Descend – ourselves to make a couch – for whom?

Ah, make the most of what we yet may spend,
Before we too into the dust descend;
Dust unto dust, and under dust to lie,
Sans wine, sans song, sans singer, – and sans End!

translated by Edward FitzGerald

A Rubáiyát is a verse of four lines. Omar Khayyám was a Persian astronomer who lived nine hundred years ago. Jump seven hundred years and Edward FitzGerald translated his verses. The whole Rubáiyát has become one of the most popular and best-selling poems in English. Most people know at least some lines from it.

blows: blossoms
Caesar: any Roman emperor
fledges: covers, adorns
vintage: harvest
sans: without

 79

High Flight

Oh! I have slipped the surly bonds of Earth
And danced the skies on laughter-silvered wings;
Sunward I've climbed, and joined the tumbling mirth
Of sun-split clouds – and done a hundred things
You have not dreamed of – wheeled and soared and
   swung
High in the sunlit silence. Hov'ring there,
I've chased the shouting wind along, and flung
My eager craft through footless halls of air...
Up, up the long, delirious, burning blue
I've topped the wind-swept heights with easy grace,
Where never lark, nor even eagle flew–
And, while with silent, lifting mind I've trod
The high untrespassed sanctity of space,
Put out my hand and touched the face of God.

John Magee

untrespassed sanctity: unspoiled holiness

Boy at the Window

Seeing the snowman standing all alone
In dusk and cold is more than he can bear.
The small boy weeps to hear the wind prepare
A night of gnashings and enormous moan.
His tearful sight can hardly reach to where
The pale-faced figure with bitumen eyes
Returns him such a god-forsaken stare
As outcast Adam gave to Paradise.

The man of snow is, nonetheless, content,
Having no wish to go inside and die.
Still, he is moved to see the youngster cry.
Though frozen water is his element,
He melts enough to drop from one soft eye
A trickle of the purest rain, a tear
For the child at the bright pane surrounded by
Such warmth, such light, such love, and so much fear.

Richard Wilbur

bitumen: *coal*

'As outcast Adam gave to Paradise.' The Bible tells the story of how Adam and Eve were thrown out of the perfect Garden of Eden.

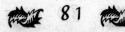

Song

Goe, and catche a falling starre,
   Get with child a mandrake roote,
Tell me, where all past yeares are,
   Or who cleft the Divels foot,
Teach me to heare Mermaides singing,
   Or to keep off envies stinging,
        And finde
        What winde
Serves to advance an honest minde.

If thou beest borne to strange sights,
   Things invisible to see,
Ride ten thousand daies and nights,
   Till age snow white haires on thee,
Thou, when thou retorn'st, wilt tell mee
All strange wonders that befell thee,
        And sweare
        No where
Lives a woman true, and faire.

If thou findst one, let mee know,
   Such a Pilgrimage were sweet;
Yet doe not, I would not goe,
   Though at next doore wee might meet,
Though shee were true, when you met her,
And last, till you write your letter,
      Yet shee
      Will bee
False, ere I come, to two, or three.

John Donne

---

mandrake: *a supposedly magical plant, whose root looks like a human*
cleft: *split (into the 'cloven hoof' that always gives him away as the devil)*
winde: *wind*

To Henrietta,
on Her Departure for Calais

When little people go abroad, wherever they may roam,
They will not just be treated as they used to be at home;
So take a few promiscuous hints, to warn you in advance,
Of how a little English girl will perhaps be served in
  France.

Of course you will be Frenchified; and first, it's my belief,
They'll dress you in their foreign style as à-la-mode as
  beef,
With a little row of bee-hives, as a border to your frock,
And a pair of frilly trousers, like a little bantam cock.

But first they'll seize your bundle (if you have one) in
  a crack,
And tie it, with a tape, by way of bustle on your back;
And make your waist so high or low, your shape will
  be a riddle,
For anyhow you'll never have your middle in the middle.

Your little English sandals for a while will hold together,
But woe betide you when the stones have worn away
  the leather;
For they'll poke your little pettitoes (and there will be
  a hobble!)
In such a pair of shoes as none but carpenters can cobble!

You'll have to learn a *chou* is quite another sort of thing
To that you put your foot in; that a *belle* is not to ring;
That a *corne* is not the knubble that brings trouble to
    your toes,
Nor *peut-être* a potato, as some Irish folks suppose.

But pray, at meals, remember this, the French are so
    polite,
No matter what you eat and drink, 'whatever is, is right'!
So when you're told at dinner time that some delicious
    stew
Is cat instead of rabbit, you must answer, '*Tant mi-eux*'!

Thomas Hood

promiscuous: here, this means haphazard or casual
à-la-mode: right in fashion (there is a dish called beef à la mode)
bustle: the cushion fancy ladies used as padding at the back
chou: French for cabbage
belle: French for a beauty
corne: French for horn
peut-être: French for perhaps (it does sound a bit like potato)
Tant mieux: French for 'even better' (but it can be made to sound like a cat's
miaow as well).

Sindhi Woman

Barefoot through the bazaar,
and with the same undulant grace
as the cloth blown back from her face,
she glides with a stone jar
high on her head
and not a ripple in her tread.

Watching her cross erect
stones, garbage, excrement, and crumbs
of glass in the Karachi slums,
I, with my stoop, reflect
they stand most straight
who learn to walk beneath a weight.

Jon Stallworthy

undulant: like a wave
excrement: human waste
Karachi: a city in Pakistan

Village Before Sunset

There is a moment country children know
When half across the field the shadows go
And even the birds sing leisurely and slow.

There's timelessness in every passing tread;
Even the far-off train as it puffs ahead,
Even the voices calling them to bed.

Frances Cornford

Old

I'm afraid of needles.
I'm tired of rubber sheets and tubes.
I'm tired of faces that I don't know
and now I think that death is starting.
Death starts like a dream,
full of objects and my sister's laughter.
We are young and we are walking
and picking wild blueberries
all the way to Damariscotta.
Oh Susan, she cried,
you've stained your new waist.
Sweet taste –
my mouth so full
and the sweet blue running out
all the way to Damariscotta.
What are you doing? Leave me alone!
Can't you see I'm dreaming?
In a dream you are never eighty.

Anne Sexton

waist: old American word for the top she's wearing

Yew Tree Guest House

In guest-house lounges
elderly ladies shrivel away
wearing bright beads and jumpers
to colour the waiting day
between breakfast and bed.

Grey widows whose beds and meals are made,
husbands tidied with the emptied cupboards,
live in mortgaged time
disguising inconsequence
with shavings of surface talk, letters
to nieces, stitches dropped in the quick-knit jacket,
picked up for makeweight meaning.

Weekdays are patterned by meals –
sole chance for speculation –
will it be cabbage or peas; boiled fish or fried?
Dead Sunday is dedicated to roast beef –
knives and forks are grips upon existence.
This diversion lengthens the journey;
and since Mrs Porter ceased to come downstairs,
ceased altogether,
the ladies at the Yew Tree Guest House
draw closer to the table.

Phoebe Hesketh

diversion: distraction, amusement

from 'In Memoriam'

Ring out, wild bells, to the wild sky,
The flying cloud, the frosty light:
The year is dying in the night;
Ring out, wild bells, and let him die.

Ring out the old, ring in the new,
Ring, happy bells, across the snow:
The year is going, let him go;
Ring out the false, ring in the true.

Ring out the grief that saps the mind,
For those that here we see no more;
Ring out the feud of rich and poor,
Ring in redress to all mankind.

Ring out a slowly dying cause,
And ancient forms of party strife;
Ring in the nobler modes of life,
With sweeter manners, purer laws.

Ring out the want, the care, the sin,
The faithless coldness of the times;
Ring out, ring out my mournful rhymes
But ring the fuller minstrel in.

 90

Ring out false pride in place and blood,
The civic slander and the spite;
Ring in the love of truth and right,
Ring in the common love of good.

Ring out old shapes of foul disease;
Ring out the narrowing lust of gold;
Ring out the thousand wars of old,
Ring in the thousand years of peace.

Ring in the valiant man and free,
The larger heart, the kindlier hand;
Ring out the darkness of the land,
Ring in the Christ that is to be.

Alfred, Lord Tennyson

saps: weakens
redress: put things to rights
party strife: political bickering
want and care: neediness and trouble
civic slander: people's lies

Pisgah-Sights

Over the ball of it,
Peering and prying,
How I see all of it,
Life there, outlying!
Roughness and smoothness,
Shine and defilement,
Grace and uncouthness:
One reconcilement.

Orbed as appointed,
Sister with brother
Joins, ne'er disjointed
One from the other.
All's lend-and-borrow;
Good, see, wants evil,
Joy demands sorrow,
Angel weds devil!

'Which things must – *why* be?'
Vain our endeavour!
So shall things aye be
As they were ever.
'Such things should *so* be!'
Sage our desistence!
Rough-smooth let globe be,
Mixed – man's existence!

Man – wise and foolish,
Lover and scorner,
Docile and mulish –
Keep each his corner!
Honey yet gall of it!
There's the life lying,
And I see all of it,
Only, I'm dying!

Robert Browning

Maybe the sheer hotchpotch of life does seem to make a sort of sense – on one's deathbed!

(The title of this poem is significant. In the Bible story, Pisgah is the mountain peak from which Moses, dying of old age after leading his people for years in the wilderness, finally saw the Promised Land – only to be told by God he would never reach it.)

And here's more on the same theme:

The Quest for Wisdom

To everything there is a season,
   and a time to every purpose under heaven.
A time to be born, and a time to die.
A time to plant, and a time to pluck up what
   is planted.
A time to kill, and a time to heal.
A time to break down, and a time to build up.
A time to weep and a time to laugh.
A time to mourn, and a time to dance.
A time to cast away stones, and a time to
   gather stones together.
A time to embrace, and a time to refrain
   from embracing.
A time to seek, and a time to lose.
A time to keep, and a time to cast away.
A time to rend, and a time to sew.
A time to keep silence, and a time to speak.
A time to love, and a time to hate.
A time of war, and a time of peace.

Ecclesiastes 3: 1–9

Ecclesiastes is one of the books in the Bible, and supposedly written by King Solomon. It means 'The Preacher'. This is one of the best-known and best-loved passages in the Old Testament.

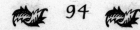

The Trees

The trees are coming into leaf
Like something almost being said;
The recent buds relax and spread,
Their greenness is a kind of grief.

Is it that they are born again
And we grow old? No, they die too.
Their yearly trick of looking new
Is written down in rings of grain.

Yet still the unresting castles thresh
In fullgrown thickness every May.
Last year is dead, they seem to say,
Begin afresh, afresh, afresh.

Philip Larkin

The Song Against Grocers

God made the wicked Grocer
For a mystery and a sign,
That men might shun the awful shops
And go to inns to dine;
Where the bacon's on the rafter
And the wine is in the wood,
And God that made good laughter
Has seen that they are good.

The evil-hearted Grocer
Would call his mother 'Ma'am',
And bow at her and bob at her,
Her aged soul to damn,
And rub his horrid hands and ask
What article was next,
Though *mortis in articulo*
Should be her proper text.

His props are not his children,
But pert lads underpaid,
Who call out 'Cash!' and bang about
To work his wicked trade;
He keeps a lady in a cage
Most cruelly all day,
And makes her count and calls her 'Miss'
Until she fades away.

The righteous minds of innkeepers
Induce them now and then
To crack a bottle with a friend
Or treat unmoneyed men,
But who hath seen the Grocer
Treat housemaids to his teas
Or crack a bottle of fish-sauce
Or stand a man a cheese?

He sells us sands of Araby
As sugar for cash down;
He sweeps his shop and sells the dust
The purest salt in town,
He crams with cans of poisoned meat
Poor subjects of the King,
And when they die by thousands
Why, he laughs like anything.

The wicked Grocer groces
In spirits and in wine,
Not frankly and in fellowship
As men in inns do dine;
But packed with soap and sardines
And carried off by grooms,
For to be snatched by Duchesses
And drunk in dressing-rooms.

The hell-instructed Grocer
Has a temple made of tin,
And the ruin of good innkeepers
Is loudly urged therein;
But now the sands are running out
From sugar of a sort,
The Grocer trembles; for his time,
Just like his weight, is short.

G. K. Chesterton

in the wood: in the barrel

mortis in articulo: at the point of death

props: helpers

a lady in a cage: in an old-fashioned grocer's the person you paid sat in a little kiosk

short weight: not as much as it should be

from A Shropshire Lad

II

Loveliest of trees, the cherry now
Is hung with bloom along the bough,
And stands about the woodland ride
Wearing white for Eastertide.

Now, of my threescore years and ten,
Twenty will not come again,
And take from seventy springs a score,
It only leaves me fifty more.

And since to look at things in bloom
Fifty springs are little room,
About the woodlands I will go
To see the cherry hung with snow.

A. E. Housman

from Cymbeline

(Act IV, Scene ii)

Fear no more the heat o' the sun,
    Nor the furious winter's rages;
Thou thy worldly task hast done,
    Home art gone, and ta'en thy wages:
Golden lads and girls all must,
As chimney-sweepers, come to dust.

Fear no more the frown o' the great,
    Thou art past the tyrant's stroke;
Care no more to clothe and eat;
    To thee the reed is as the oak:
The sceptre, learning, physic, must
All follow this, and come to dust.

Fear no more the lightning-flash,
    Nor the all-dreaded thunder-stone;
Fear not slander, censure rash;
    Thou hast finished joy and moan:
All lovers young, all lovers must,
Consign to thee, and come to dust.

William Shakespeare

Nothing can touch you once you're dead.

'sceptre, learning, physic' is a poetical way of saying 'even kings, wise men and doctors'
'slander, censure rash': lies and unfair criticism
consign: submit, give in

Francis

Today you told me how the wind
Frightened the washing and yesterday
When we sat down to picnic
In a shining field of hay
You said you could not eat because
You'd swallowed so much sun.
I scratch and grub to make from wind and hay
My ill-shaped cups to catch a little sun.
Perhaps I should put down my pen
And close my eyes and let you spill
Your careless poems in my lap.

Susan Hamlyn

The poet's saying that she has to strain to find the vivid images that crop up so naturally in her young son's chatter.

The Aunties

Do you remember the dances, the candles,
the beaux and the carriages, fans and scarves?

We forget nothing, that's our trouble,
and every day there's more to remember
so that things to remember lie around us
like cobwebs in drifts and we hear the voices
and what they say.

The sounds break over us like blue waves
over ancient rocks and like blue waves the voices
leave a foam behind that froths like lace at first,
hardening later into memories.

Adèle Geras

beaux: young men

Grannie

I stayed with her when I was six then went
To live elsewhere when I was eight years old.
For ages I remembered her faint scent
Of lavender, the way she'd never scold
No matter what I'd done, and most of all
The way her smile seemed, somehow, to enfold
My whole world like a warm, protective shawl.

I knew that I was safe when she was near,
She was so tall, so wide, so large, she would
Stand mountainous between me and my fear,
Yet oh, so gentle, and she understood
Every hope and dream I ever had.
She praised me lavishly when I was good,
But never punished me when I was bad.

Years later war broke out and I became
A soldier and was wounded while in France.
Back home in hospital, still very lame,
I realized suddenly that circumstance
Had brought me close to that small town where she
Was living still. And so I seized the chance
To write and ask if she could visit me.

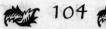

She came. And I still vividly recall
The shock that I received when she appeared
That dark cold day. Huge grannie was so small!
A tiny, frail, old lady. It was weird.
She hobbled through the ward to where I lay
And drew quite close and, hesitating, peered.
And then she smiled: and love lit up the day.

Vernon Scannell

The donkey wouldn't win any animal beauty parades, but the one in this next poem is reminding us that Christ did choose him to ride on in triumph into Jerusalem, when, as a gesture of welcome and respect, the people cried 'Hosanna!' and threw palm leaves on the streets in front of them.

The Donkey

When fishes flew and forests walked
    And figs grew upon thorn,
Some moment when the moon was blood
    Then surely I was born;

With monstrous head and sickening cry
    And ears like errant wings,
The devil's walking parody
    On all four-footed things.

The tattered outlaw of the earth,
    Of ancient crooked will;
Starve, scourge, deride me: I am dumb,
    I keep my secret still.

Fools! For I also had my hour;
    One far fierce hour and sweet:
There was a shout about my ears,
    And palms before my feet.

G. K. Chesterton

errant: gone wrong
parody: joke version
ancient crooked will: famously stubborn
scourge, deride me: whip me, scoff at me

Poetry

When they say
That every day
Men die miserably without it:
I doubt it.

I have known several men and women
Replete with the stuff
Who died quite miserably
Enough.

And to hear of the human race's antennae!
Then I
Wonder what human race
They have in mind.
One of the poets I most admire
Is blind,
For instance. You wouldn't trust him
To lead you to the Gents:
Let alone through the future tense.

And unacknowledged legislators!
How's that for insane afflatus?
Not one I've met
Is the sort of bore
To wish to draft a law.

No,

I like what vamped me
In my youth:
Tune, argument,
Colour, truth.

Kit Wright

Poets have been called 'the human race's antennae' and our 'unacknowledged legislators'. This poet's not impressed by that sort of talk.

replete: filled
insane afflatus: a madly puffed-up idea
vamped: seduced, enchanted

Romance

When I was but thirteen or so
  I went into a golden land;
Chimborazo, Cotopaxi
  Took me by the hand.

My father died, my brother too,
  They passed like fleeting dreams.
I stood where Popocatapetl
  In the sunlight gleams.

I dimly heard the Master's voice
  And boys far off at play,
Chimborazo, Cotopaxi
  Had stolen me away.

I walked in a great golden dream
  To and fro from school –
Shining Popocatapetl
  The dusty streets did rule.

I walked home with a gold dark boy
  And never a word I'd say;
Chimborazo, Cotopaxi
  Had taken my speech away:

I gazed entranced upon his face
   Fairer than any flower –
O shining Popocatapetl
   It was thy magic hour:

The houses, people, traffic seemed
   Thin fading dreams by day,
Chimborazo, Cotopaxi
   They had stolen my soul away!

Walter James Turner

Chimborazo, Cotopaxi and Popocatapetl are volcanoes. The first two are in Ecuador, the last in Mexico.

To School!

Let all the little poets be gathered together in classes
And let prizes be given to them by the Prize Asses
And let them be sure to call all the little poets young
And worse follow what's bad begun
But do not expect the Muse to attend this school
Why look already how far off she has flown, she is no
    fool.

Stevie Smith

the Muse: the goddess who inspires poets

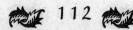

School Buses

You'd think that by the end of June they'd take
  themselves
Away, get out of sight – but no, they don't; they
Don't at all. You see them waiting through
July in clumps of sumac near the railroad, or
Behind a service station, watching, always watching
  for a
Child who's let go of summer's hand and strayed. I have
Seen them hunting on the roads of August – empty buses
Scanning woods and ponds with rows of empty eyes.
  This morning
I saw five of them, parked like a week of
Schooldays, smiling slow in orange paint and
Smirking with their mirrors in the sun –
But summer isn't done! Not yet!

Russell Hoban

sumacs are leafy shrubs

The poet means those yellowish school buses you see in American films.

On Setting My Class Their First Quiz

Fifty-three faces, sad and apprehensive,
The boys in jeans attired, with flat-topped hair,
The girls more gaily dressed, and more expensive –
More frightening, and more fair –

All sit with pen in hand and book on knee,
Prepared to write, uncertain what to say,
All hating Coleridge, and loathing me,
Wishing the hour away.

My dears, I will not quiz you any more,
You shall be graded only for your faces . . .
You, sirs, I'll grade for patience and cropped skull.

I never passed so long an hour before! –
But surely somewhere in you there are traces
Of Blake and Wordsworth, though I make them dull?

Kenneth Hopkins

Coleridge, Blake and Wordsworth: all three come up next. See what you think.

 114

Under the effects of opium, Coleridge fell asleep and dreamed a poem. On waking, he managed to write this much – about a third of it – before he was interrupted by a visitor who has gone down in history as 'the person from Porlock'. This phrase is now used as a joke to refer to anyone who stops a creative artist getting on with it.

Kubla Khan

In Xanadu did Kubla Khan
   A stately pleasure-dome decree:
Where Alph, the sacred river, ran
Through caverns measureless to man
   Down to a sunless sea.
So twice five miles of fertile ground
   With walls and towers were girdled round:
And there were gardens bright with sinuous rills
Where blossomed many an incense-bearing tree;
And here were forests ancient as the hills,
Enfolding sunny spots of greenery.

But O! that deep romantic chasm which slanted
Down the green hill athwart a cedarn cover!
A savage place! As holy and enchanted
As e'er beneath a waning moon was haunted
By woman wailing for her demon-lover!
And from this chasm, with ceaseless turmoil seething,
As if this earth in fast thick pants were breathing,
A mighty fountain momently was forced;
Amid whose swift half-intermitted burst
Huge fragments vaulted like rebounding hail,

Or chaffy grain beneath the thresher's flail:
And 'mid these dancing rocks at once and ever
It flung up momently the sacred river.
Five miles meandering with a mazy motion
Through wood and dale the sacred river ran,
Then reached the caverns measureless to man,
And sank in tumult to a lifeless ocean:
And 'mid this tumult Kubla heard from far
Ancestral voices prophesying war!

    The shadow of the dome of pleasure
       Floated midway on the waves;
    Where was heard the mingled measure
       From the fountain and the caves.
  It was a miracle of rare device,
 A sunny pleasure-dome with caves of ice!

    A damsel with a dulcimer
       In a vision once I saw:
    It was an Abyssinian maid,
       And on her dulcimer she played,
    Singing of Mount Abora.
    Could I revive within me,
    Her symphony and song,

To such a deep delight 'twould win me,

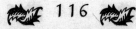

That with music loud and long,
I would build that dome in air,
That sunny dome! those caves of ice!
And all who heard should see them there,
And all should cry, Beware! Beware!
His flashing eyes, his floating hair!
  Weave a circle round him thrice,
   And close your eyes with holy dread,
   For he on honey-dew hath fed,
  And drunk the milk of Paradise.

Samuel Taylor Coleridge

sinuous rills: winding streams
momently: in an instant
intermitted: on and off
rebounding: bouncing
chaffy grain: wheat with husks flying off
measure: here, this means sounds of water
damsel: young maiden
dulcimer: stringed instrument

And Did Those Feet in Ancient Time

And did those feet in ancient time
Walk upon England's mountains green?
And was the holy lamb of God
On England's pleasant pastures seen?

And did the countenance divine
Shine forth upon our clouded hills?
And was Jerusalem builded here
Among those dark satanic mills?

Bring me my bow of burning gold:
Bring me my arrows of desire:
Bring me my spear: O clouds unfold!
Bring me my chariot of fire.

I will not cease from mental fight,
Nor shall my sword sleep in my hand
Till we have built Jerusalem
In England's green and pleasant land.

William Blake

Blake's poetry is 'mystical' (religiously weird). The 'holy lamb of God' means Christ. The 'dark satanic mills' is thought to refer to the universities, churning out teachings of which Blake disapproved, and the whole poem is really a plea to return to a Christly spirit. Most people know this as a hymn, and sooner or later you'll have to sing it at someone's funeral.

Lucy Gray; or, Solitude

Oft I had heard of Lucy Gray:
And, when I crossed the wild,
I chanced to see at break of day
The solitary child.

No mate, no comrade Lucy knew;
She dwelt on a wide moor,
– The sweetest thing that ever grew
Beside a human door!

You yet may spy the fawn at play,
The hare upon the green;
But the sweet face of Lucy Gray
Will never more be seen.

'Tonight will be a stormy night –
You to the town must go;
And take a lantern, child, to light
Your mother through the snow.'

'That, Father, will I gladly do:
'Tis scarcely afternoon –
The minster-clock has just struck two,
And yonder is the moon!'

At this the father raised his hook,
And snapped a faggot-band;
He plied his work; and Lucy took
The lantern in her hand.

Not blither is the mountain roe:
With many a wanton stroke
Her feet disperse the powdery snow,
That rises up like smoke.

The storm came on before its time:
She wandered up and down;
And many a hill did Lucy climb:
But never reached the town.

The wretched parents all that night
Went shouting far and wide;
But there was neither sound nor sight
To serve them for a guide.

At daybreak on a hill they stood
That overlooked the moor;
And thence they saw the bridge of wood,
A furlong from their door.

They wept – and, turning homeward, cried
'In heaven we all shall meet!'
– When in the snow the mother spied
The print of Lucy's feet.

Then downwards from the steep hill's edge
They tracked the footmarks small;
And through the broken hawthorn hedge,
And by the long stone-wall:

And then an open field they crossed,
The marks were still the same;
They tracked them on, nor ever lost;
And to the bridge they came:

They followed from the snowy bank
Those footmarks, one by one,
Into the middle of the plank;
And further there were none!

– Yet some maintain that to this day
She is a living child;
That you may see sweet Lucy Gray
Upon the lonesome wild.

O'er rough and smooth she trips along,
And never looks behind;
And sings a solitary song
That whistles in the wind.

William Wordsworth

faggot-band: bundle of sticks
blither: carefree
wanton: here this means playful

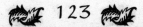

Full Moon and Little Frieda

A cool small evening shrunk to a dog bark and the
   clank of a bucket –

And you listening.
A spider's web, tense for the dew's touch.
A pail lifted, still and brimming – mirror
To tempt a first star to tremor.

Cows are going home in the lane there, looping the
   hedges with their warm wreaths of breath –
A dark river of blood, many boulders,
Balancing unspilled milk.

'Moon!' you cry suddenly, 'Moon! Moon!'

The moon has stepped back like an artist gazing
   amazed at a work
That points at him amazed.

Ted Hughes

from The Song of Hiawatha

Here's a part of the famous original. Hiawatha, against advice, sets out to find his missing father. I've explained some of the possibly unfamiliar words over the page at the end.

IV: Hiawatha and Mudjekeewis

. . . From his lodge went Hiawatha,
Dressed for travel, armed for hunting;
Dressed in deer-skin shirt and leggings,
Richly wrought with quills and wampum;
On his head his eagle-feathers,
Round his waist his belt of wampum,
In his hand his bow of ash-wood,
Strung with sinews of the reindeer;
In his quiver oaken arrows,
Tipped with jasper, winged with feathers;
With his mittens, Minjekahwun,
With his moccasins enchanted.
Warning said the old Nokomis,
'Go not forth, O Hiawatha!
To the kingdom of the West-Wind,
To the realms of Mudjekeewis,
Lest he harm you with his magic,
Lest he kill you with his cunning!'
But the fearless Hiawatha
Heeded not her woman's warning;
Forth he strode into the forest,
At each stride a mile he measured;

Lurid seemed the sky above him,
Lurid seemed the earth beneath him,
Hot and close the air around him,
Filled with smoke and fiery vapours,
As of burning wood and prairies,
For his heart was hot within him,
Like a living coal his heart was.

So he journeyed westward, westward,
Left the fleetest deer behind him,
Left the antelope and bison;
Crossed the rushing Esconawhaw,
Crossed the mighty Mississippi.
Passed the Mountains of the Prairie,
Passed the land of Crows and Foxes,
Passed the dwellings of the Blackfeet,
Came unto the Rocky Mountains,
To the kingdom of the West-Wind,
Where upon the gusty summits
Salt the ancient Mudjekeewis,
Ruler of the winds of heaven.

Filled with awe was Hiawatha
At the aspect of his father.
On the air about him wildly
Tossed and streamed his cloudy tresses,
Gleamed like drifting snow his tresses,
Glared like Ishkoodah, the comet,
Like the star with fiery tresses.

Filled with joy was Mudjekeewis
When he looked on Hiawatha,
Saw his youth rise up before him

In the face of Hiawatha,
Saw the beauty of Wenonah
From the grave rise up before him.
   'Welcome!' said he, 'Hiawatha,
To the kingdom of the West-Wind!
Long have I been waiting for you!
Youth is lovely, age is lonely,
Youth is fiery, age is frosty;
You bring back the days departed,
You bring back my youth of passion,
And the beautiful Wenonah!'
   Many days they talked together,
Questioned, listened, waited, answered;
Much the mighty Mudjekeewis
Boasted of his ancient prowess,
Of his perilous adventures,
His indomitable courage,
His invulnerable body.
   Patiently sat Hiawatha,
Listening to his father's boasting;
With a smile he sat and listened,
Uttered neither threat nor menace,
Neither word nor look betrayed him,
But his heart was hot within him,
Like a living coal his heart was.

Henry Wadsworth Longfellow

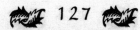

wampum: beads made of shells, used as money
realms: lands
lurid: vivid, glowing
aspect: appearance
tresses: hair
prowess: skills
perilous: dangerous
indomitable: unbeatable
invulnerable: can't be wounded

And here's the spoof, or parody, all written in Longfellow's famously distinctive verse rhythm. Again, I've added explanations of some words at the end of the poem.

Hiawatha's Photographing

From his shoulder Hiawatha
Took the camera of rosewood,
Made of sliding, folding rosewood;
Neatly put it all together.
In its case it lay compactly,
Folded into nearly nothing;

But he opened out the hinges,
Pushed and pulled the joints and hinges,
Till it looked all squares and oblongs,
Like a complicated figure
In the Second Book of Euclid.

This he perched upon a tripod –
Crouched beneath its dusky cover –
Stretched his hand, enforcing silence –
Said, 'Be motionless, I beg you!'
Mystic, awful was the process.

All the family in order
Sat before him for their pictures:
Each in turn, as he was taken,
Volunteered his own suggestions,
His ingenious suggestions.

First the Governor, the Father:
He suggested velvet curtains
Looped about a massy pillar;
And the corner of a table,
Of a rosewood dining-table.

He would hold a scroll of something,
Hold it firmly in his left-hand;
He would keep his right-hand buried
(Like Napoleon) in his waistcoat;
He would contemplate the distance
With a look of pensive meaning,
As of ducks that die in tempests.

Grand, heroic was the notion:
Yet the picture failed entirely:
Failed, because he moved a little,
Moved, because he couldn't help it.

Next, his better half took courage;
She would have her picture taken.
She came dressed beyond description,
Dressed in jewels and in satin
Far too gorgeous for an empress.
Gracefully she sat down sideways,
With a simper scarcely human,
Holding in her hand a bouquet
Rather larger than a cabbage.
All the while that she was sitting,

Still the lady chattered, chattered,
Like a monkey in the forest.
'Am I sitting still?' she asked him.
'Is my face enough in profile?
Shall I hold the bouquet higher?
Will it come into the picture?'
And the picture failed completely.

Next the Son, the Stunning-Cantab:
He suggested curves of beauty,
Curves pervading all his figure,
Which the eye might follow onward,
Till they centred in the breast-pin,
Centred in the golden breast-pin.
He had learnt it all from Ruskin
(Author of 'The Stones of Venice',
'Seven Lamps of Architecture',
'Modern Painters', and some others);
And perhaps he had not fully
Understood his author's meaning;
But, whatever was the reason,
All was fruitless, as the picture
Ended in an utter failure.

Next to him the eldest daughter:
She suggested very little,
Only asked if he would take her
With her look of 'passive beauty'.

Her idea of passive beauty
Was a squinting of the left-eye,
Was a drooping of the right-eye,
Was a smile that went up sideways
To the corner of the nostrils.

Hiawatha, when she asked him,
Took no notice of the question,
Looked as if he hadn't heard it;
But, when pointedly appealed to,
Smiled in his peculiar manner,
Coughed and said it 'didn't matter',
Bit his lip and changed the subject.

Nor in this was he mistaken,
As the picture failed completely.

So in turn the other sisters.

Last, the youngest son was taken:
Very rough and thick his hair was,
Very round and red his face was,
Very dusty was his jacket,
Very fidgety his manner.
And his overbearing sisters
Called him names he disapproved of:
Called him Johnny, 'Daddy's Darling',
Called him Jacky, 'Scrubby School-boy'.
And, so awful was the picture,
In comparison the others

Seemed, to one's bewildered fancy,
To have partially succeeded.

Finally my Hiawatha
Tumbled all the tribe together,
('Grouped' is not the right expression),
And, as happy chance would have it
Did at last obtain a picture
Where the faces all succeeded:
Each came out a perfect likeness.

Then they joined and all abused it,
Unrestrainedly abused it,
As the worst and ugliest picture
They could possibly have dreamed of.
'Giving one such strange expressions –
Sullen, stupid, pert expressions.
Really any one would take us
(Any one that did not know us)
For the most unpleasant people!'
(Hiawatha seemed to think so,
Seemed to think it not unlikely).
All together rang their voices,
Angry, loud, discordant voices,
As of dogs that howl in concert,
As of cats that wail in chorus.

But my Hiawatha's patience,
His politeness and his patience,
Unaccountably had vanished,

And he left that happy party.
Neither did he leave them slowly,
With the calm deliberation,
The intense deliberation
Of a photographic artist:
But he left them in a hurry,
Left them in a mighty hurry,
Stating that he would not stand it,
Stating in emphatic language
What he'd be before he'd stand it.
Hurriedly he packed his boxes:
Hurriedly the porter trundled
On a barrow all his boxes:
Hurriedly he took his ticket:
Hurriedly the train received him:
Thus departed Hiawatha.

Lewis Carroll

Book of Euclid: geometry book (v. hard)
tripod: three-legged stand
awful: impressive, awesome
ingenious: clever
pensive: thoughtful
better half: wife
abused it: were rude about it
deliberation: unhurriedness

emphatic: strong
in profile: sideways
Cantab: student at Cambridge

Never, My Love and Dearest

Never, my love and dearest,
    we'll hear the lilies grow
or, silent and dancing,
    the fall of the winter snow,
or the great clouds of Summer
    as on their way they go.

Never, my love and dearest,
    we'll hear the bluebells chime
or the whole world turn over
    after the starlit time.
O not everything, my dearest,
    needs to be said in rhyme!

George Barker

The Curtain

When the curtain goes down at the end of the play,
The actors and actresses hurry away.

Titania, Bottom, and Quince, being stars,
Can afford to drive home in their own private cars.

Hippolyta, Starveling, and Flute are in luck,
They've been offered a lift in a taxi by Puck;

And Snug and Lysander and Oberon pop
In a bus, and Demetrius clambers on top.

With the chorus of fairies no bus can compete,
So they are obliged to trudge home on their feet:

It seems rather hard on the poor little things,
After flying about all the evening with wings.

Guy Boas

The play is Shakespeare's A Midsummer Night's Dream.

A Book

There is no frigate like a book
    To take us lands away,
Nor any coursers like a page
    Of prancing poetry.
This traverse may the poorest take
    Without oppress of toll;
How frugal is the chariot
    That bears a human soul!

Emily Dickinson

frigate: ship
courser: swift horse
traverse: road
oppress of toll: having to pay
frugal: simple and cheap

Index of Titles/First Lines

Index of Poets

145

Acknowledgements

The publishers and the compiler thank the following for permission to reprint copyright material:

John Agard, 'Come From That Window Child' from *Mangoes and Bullets* (Pluto Press, 1985), copyright © John Agard, 1985; reprinted by permission of the Caroline Sheldon Literary Agency.

W. H. Auden, 'O What Is That Sound?' from *Collected Poems* (Faber and Faber, 1976), copyright © Edward Mendelson, William Meredith and Monroe K. Spears, executors of the Estate of W. H. Auden, 1976; reprinted by permission of Faber and Faber.

George Barker, 'You Many Big Ships With Your Billowing Sails' and 'Never, My Love and Dearest' from *Runes and Rhymes* (Faber and Faber, 1969), copyright © George Barker, 1969; reprinted by permission of Faber and Faber.

Hilaire Belloc, 'Tarantella' from *Complete Verse* (Pimlico, 1991), copyright © the Estate of Hilaire Belloc, 1970; reprinted by permission of Peters, Fraser and Dunlop Ltd on behalf of the Estate of Hilaire Belloc.

James Berry, 'Okay, Brown Girl, Okay' from *Playing a Dazzler* (Hamish Hamilton, 1996), copyright © James Berry, 1996; reprinted by permission of Peters, Fraser and Dunlop Ltd on behalf of the author.

John Betjeman, 'Hunter Trials' from *Collected Poems* (John Murray, 1958), copyright © John Betjeman, 1958, 1962, 1970; reprinted by permission of John Murray.

Guy Boas, 'The Curtain' from *Selected Light Verse of Guy Boas of Punch* (The Shakespeare Head, 1964), copyright © Basil Blackwell and Mott Ltd, 1964; reprinted by permission of Punch, Ltd.

G. K. Chesterton, 'The Song Against Grocers' and 'The Donkey' from *Collected Poems of G. K. Chesterton* (Methuen, 1933); reprinted by permission of A. P. Watt Ltd on behalf of the Royal Literary Fund.